Hush, Little One

A Lullaby for God's Children

Can be sung to the melody for "Hush, Little Baby"

Anita Reith Stohs

Illustrated by John Kanzler

CONCORDIA PUBLISHING HOUSE · SAINT LOUIS

For
Isabel and Margaret Safarik

May Jesus, who so loves you,

Keep you safe in His protecting arms,

This night ... and your whole life long.

Text copyright © 2002 Anita Reith Stohs

Illustrations copyright © 2002 Concordia Publishing House

Published by Concordia Publishing House

3558 S. Jefferson Avenue, St. Louis, MO 63118-3968

Manufactured in the United States of America

2	3	4	5	6	7	8	9	10	11
03	04	05	06	07	08	09	10	11	12	13

This is a special gift for

Baby Coleman

given by

Andrea

Hush, little one, don't say a word,

All your prayers by Jesus are heard.

Now it's time to climb into bed,

And lay down your sleepy head.

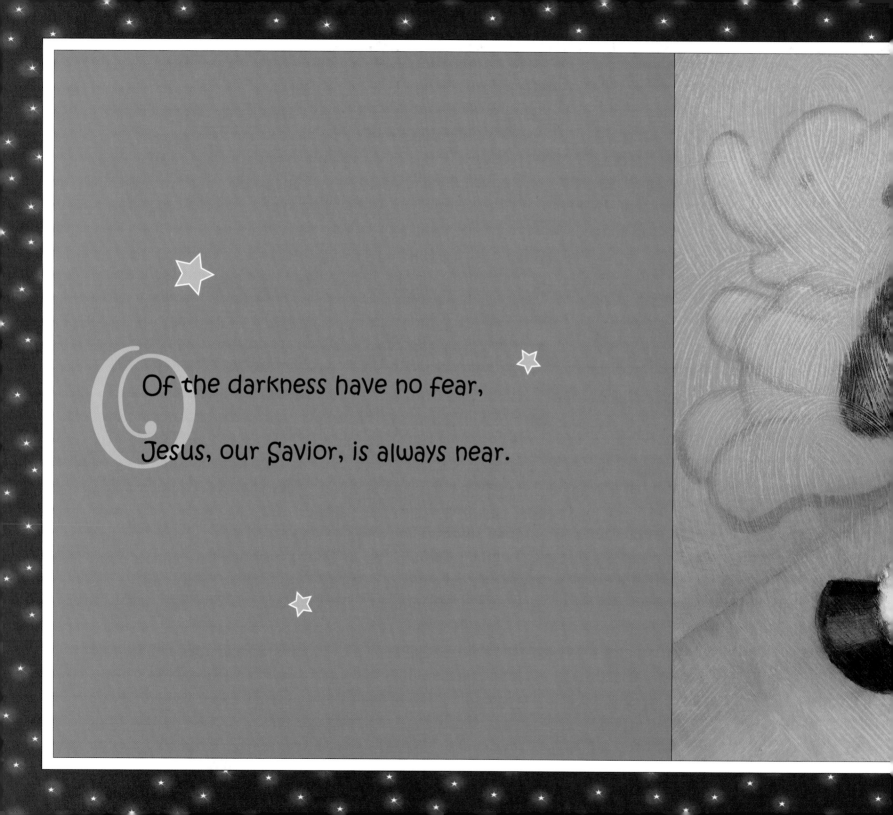

Of the darkness have no fear,

Jesus, our Savior, is always near.

He who died and rose again,

Now forgives our every sin.

Angels sent from heaven above,

Watch over you with eyes of love.

As the sun sinks in the west,

His little creatures stop to rest.

Far in the forest, a small, shy deer,

Snuggles to sleep with her mother near.

Deep in a burrow, small bunnies creep,

Close to their mother and fall asleep.

Inside the barn, on soft, fresh hay,

A newborn calf ends its very first day.

High in a tree, no chirp is heard,

From inside a nest of slumbering birds.

Curled on her rug, your mama cat purrs,

A last lullaby to those kittens of hers.

And for you, my little one,

The time to sleep has also come.

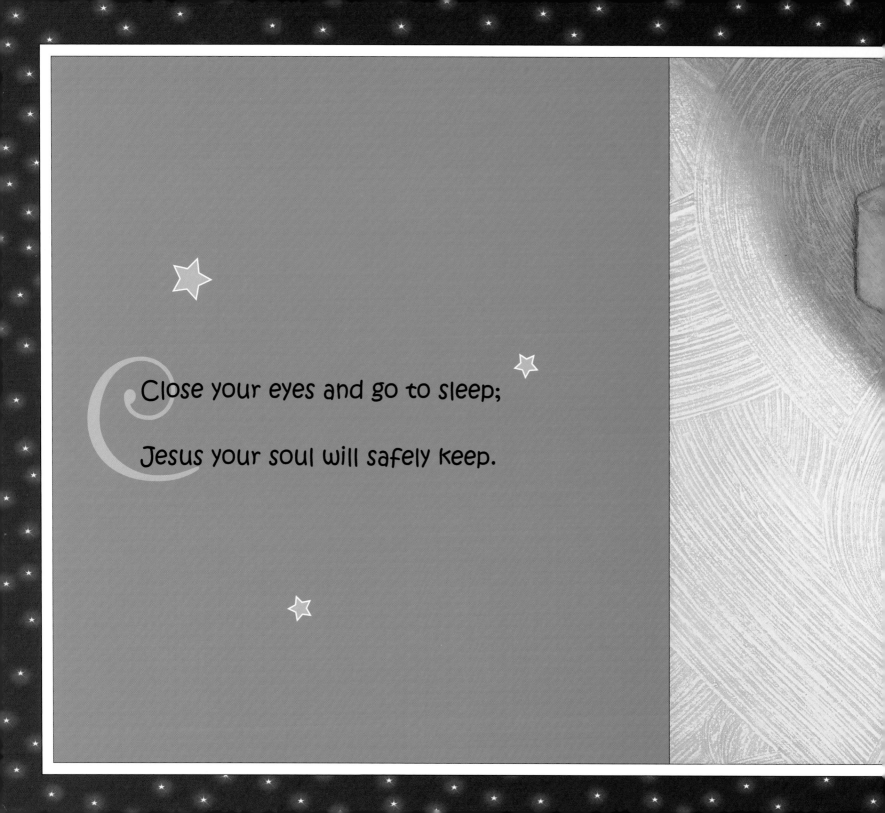

Close your eyes and go to sleep;

Jesus your soul will safely keep.

He is with you through the night,

'Til the dawn of morning light.

Nighttime has come. The evening bath is finished. Your little one is ready for a good-night story and song, as well as an evening prayer. This is a special time for you and your child to build memories that will last a lifetime.

As you pray together, thanking God for His many blessings and asking for His protection during the coming night, you are teaching your little one the importance of prayer. You are also modeling faith and trust in God. When your child later thinks back to these bedtime moments, he will remember stories you read, songs you sang, and prayers you said. Most important, he will remember your love, your attention, and your faithful example.

God uses you to reflect His unconditional love on those around you, especially your child. Through you, your child will see glimpses of God's love. Through your daily care and loving actions, she will come to appreciate what God teaches us in His Word—that He is trustworthy, that His love never ends, and that His children are safely held within His loving hands.

Thank God for the gift of your child. Ask Him to shine His love through you as your child grows in faith and love.

Anita

Bedtime or Bedlam?

The following suggestions may help turn bedtime into a blessed time for both you and your child.

1. Be consistent. Make sure your child goes to sleep and rises around the same time each day. Avoid long naps and late-afternoon naps. Keep in mind that most toddlers only need 10 hours of sleep a day.

2. Establish a consistent bedtime ritual. One example is: have a snack, use the bathroom, brush teeth, read Bible stories, then say prayers.

3. Avoid wild play right before bedtime. Excited children need additional time to settle down before sleep.

4. Read to your child from the moment he is born. Begin with board books and proceed to picture books. Include a child's Bible and a collection of Bible stories in your reading selections. It is never too early to teach these stories of God's love and faithfulness.

5. Sing lullabies, simple Jesus songs, and favorite hymns with your child. Songs sung when your child is young will stay with her the rest of her life.

6. Pray with your child. Teach standard prayers such as the Lord's Prayer and common table prayers. Invite your child to pray out loud.

7. Add a special goodnight that communicates the love of Jesus. Some examples are: "Jesus loves you, and so do I" or "May Jesus keep you safe."

The author knows the challenge of bedtime. At one time, she was tucking in three children under five years old. She sang many songs in the hallway to all of her children at once. Perhaps this book can become one for you to sing.